to Ro

Affie

BARKIN!

love from

Mike
§
(Merthyr Tudful)

Barkin!

*Poems and stories
in Merthyr dialect*

Mike Jenkins

By the same author and published by Gwasg Carreg Gwalch:

Laughter Tangled in Thorn
The Language of Flight
Walking on Waste

First published in 2013

© Mike Jenkins

© Gwasg Carreg Gwalch 2013

Published with the financial support
of the Welsh Books Council

ISBN: 978-1-84527-418-4

Cover design: Welsh Books Council

Published by Gwasg Carreg Gwalch,
12 Iard yr Orsaf, Llanrwst, Wales LL26 0EH
tel: 01492 642031
fax: 01492 641502
email: books@carreg-gwalch.com
website: www.carreg-gwalch.com

For Marie, as always,
and for Andrew,
whose favourite word is 'Barkin!'

Contents

The stories

The poems

Posh Pirate

There's a newclear scientist
lives up Dowlais Top
knows wha's goin on

an there's a pirate,
a fully-fledged buccaneer,
walkin round ower town

there's a cannon outside Cyfarthfa
an ee sits astride it,
but ee int firin nothin

there's a Council sittin an yappin
bout the colours o bags f re-cyclin
an there's a pirate oo's watchin em

there's a trolley stuck in-a river,
Taekwando at-a Leisure Centre,
but ee int sailin or fightin

coz ee's buyin a cheapo cutlass
an a small inflatable parrot
from ower very best Pound Shop

once stood 'gainst a well-known Tory,
plays on is mouth organ 'Hen Wlad Fy Nhadau',
ee knows ow to ambush poetree

picks arguments with minin engineers,
leaves nex day soon as ee can;
posh pirate leggin it to Englan'.

The girl oo become Blonde

Sittin on-a bus t Cardiff
nex to the minginest person as always,
windows shut an I'm gaggin.

Then this girl, jest by Whitchurch,
does this really weird thing
(bout 16, dressed in Chinos an Converse);

she puts a back cap over er air,
short black air an simple
not like er fren's purpley streaks an spikes;

takes out a long blonde wig
from a plastic bag an puts it on;
nobuddy bats an eye-lid.

The girl seems appy an pats er wig
an I carn elp wonderin what for:
some date with a bloke oo likes em fair?

Is it some disguise, or t make er
look a lot older in a bar?
On a bus fulla baldies and silveries

an the mankiest person in-a universe,
the girl looks more like an actress
gettin ready f'r er latest role.

I'm A Dead Man

She've left
she've gone,
to er I'm a dead man

we lived close by,
supper t'gether
an now Aberdare

might jest as well
be Australia
f'r all she cares

I paint, do collages,
end up turnin em black,
end up burnin em up

all them yers
f'r what?
no kids, no nothin!

carn even play
my mewsic no more,
I sol the television

tha Clinic turned er
'gainst me an I even
paid f'r er t be there

too many voices
when she shoulda slept:
er father fucked er up

now I'm left t regret
I couldn be er child an usban':
I'll ave a fewnral f r myself

drink till my ead's a canvas
stretched an ready f r-a brush,
but my ands shake, I carn raise it.

In Memree of 'Toilet'

Don' know why they called im that.
Not sif ee always ad a chain
danglin round is neck,
not sif ee wuz boggin.

I jest remember im, Beatles mad
an on about McCartney an Lennon
an George Arrison's great songs
ee said woz underrated.

Ewsed t see im down town buskin
an ee could always be relied on
to supply mega lush weed;
often ad a tidee girlfren with im.

With is long black air
an later a moush, yew'd swear
ee wuz part of a Beatles tribute.
One of-a many oo shoulda made it.

F'r-a time ee wuz livin
in-a Teepee village over by Carmarthen,
another ee seemed t be sortin
loadsa stuff f'r the Green Man.

I carn forget the fight ee ad
in class with Crumpy oo wuz inta Elvis,
it wuz all about mewsic, oo woz best:
don' think anybuddy lost.

Toilet. Eart-attack! So young
it don' seem right:
I'll play a song an think of im;
it's gotta be 'Blackbird singin in the dead o night'.

Las Person on-a Planet!

Couldn bleeve it when she tol me
'See im, over by there,
ee's a sex addict, a Swinger!'

Ee nodded to me – 'Orright?'
I almos coughed up my pint.
Ewsed t live opposite.

Ee wuz a twt,
ead like a ewge peanut,
goin baldy before is time.

Left is missis, twice is size,
yeard is daughter say
bout im avin a mid-life crisis.

Las person on-a planet!
Always out washin is car
or tendin to is roses.

Couldn see im as a serial shagger!
Worked as a bank clerk,
got a transfer.

Ee woz at-a counter,
'I'd like t take it out!' I sayz,
my mistake makin me splutter.

'An I always thought,' ee joked,
'yew woz a quiet one!
I wouldn do it in yer!'

Smokin the Torch

It woz an ordinree day in May
an me, Welly an Scripo bin drinkin all day;
Scripo wuz off of is face.

Somebuddy ud sol im speed
an ee wuz a manic pub screecher,
eyeballs poppin, ands like birds oppin.

The pub starts gettin fulla
an we ardly noticed, people buzzin
with – 'It's on its way!' 'It's comin!'

Jest as Scripo wuz doin
is famous impersonation of a woman givin birth,
ev'ryone charges f'r-a door like January Sales.

Welly moans – 'Not the fuckin Queen agen!'
I jump like I wuz pogoin;
Scripo dodgin t the front before I cun stop im.

Nex moment, pleece escort, this athlete
oldin a ewge gold torch come runnin.
But Scripo gets it all wrong.

Arf pissed, arf stoned, thinks it's a giant spliff,
grabs an shoves it in is gob
arfta shoutin – 'Tha's mine!'

As cops catch old of is coat
ee yells out – 'Ardest joint I ever smoked!'
Ee singed theyer eyeballs with-a flame!

They frogmarch im off an Welly starts singin
'God save the Queen, it's a fascist regime!'
ee gets arrested an I'm left alone.

In-a 'Merthyr' nex week wuz the eadline
REPUBLICAN DRUNKARDS RUIN OLYMPIC RELAY!
an I made Scripo a Yew-tube sensation.

Ewman Advert

I woz standin at-a bus stop
right by-a KFC
bastin an bakin in-a smell
of chicken fat an chip oil,
waitin f'r a number 9 t Irwin.

The low mornin sun
woz shinin straight at me,
my jacket starts cracklin,
it wuz ot as an oven,
my arms like two drumsticks.

When-a bus come
I couldn wave it down,
I woz totelee paralyzed!
A sign cross my t-shirt read –
'Colonel Sanders Needs You'
like an army recrewtment poster.

I tried t speak t passin people
an on'y come out with en noises;
theyer dog salutes is leg
an pisses all over my jeans.

The reek ad got inta my bones,
my nose a parson's,
my skin nothin but breadcrumbs.
'Ee looks delicious! I'd love t eat im!'
some kids shout, pokin
an proddin t make me cluck.

Then, sudden as it ud appened,
the wind changes direction,
clouds cover up-a sun
an rain dampens down the stinkin air.

A free man agen, I forget Irwin
an wing back up the ill
like some petrified chicken
about t ave its throat slit
an its guts bagged in plastic.

All Poetree's Gay

Wish I never wrote tha poem
coz all poetree's gay,
it's right wha they say.

All I ever done
woz scribble it down
an I won this competition.

All I got wuz book tokens anyway –
sol em t my ol man,
ee give me the money.

Int no ewse wha-a teacher sayz –
'In Wales, it's a tradition.'
An summin bout bards an-a.

I'm feelin bloody bard orright,
all-a boyz give me jip –
'Yew gay or wha?'

All it woz, wuz an ol man
stuck in-a Ome, nobuddy visitin,
moanin, 'Lissen t me. Lissen!'

When-a Ead o Yer starts droolin –
'Oo Liam, what a lovely poem!'
felt gay as fuck, felt like fightin.

Barkin!

Lately I seen im
totelee without Fancy Dress.
It's like spottin
yewer footie idol
in a suit,
or some lush model
with all er clothes on.

Ee wuz carryin
two bopa-bags
full o shoppin.
Ee wore a grey suit,
white tie an shirt
with-a hankie in-a pocket;
is silvery air
woz plastered down
in thick, greasy strands
tryin t ide is baldin,
it ung in a wiry web
right above is fore'ead.

Makes a change from D-Day Dave,
Mr Universe Dave or Crocodile DunDave
with is corky at,
or April Fool's Dave with jester bells.

I wan'ed t peek in is bags
t see if they woz full o costumes
t keep us all cleckin –
'Barkin? Ee's – a definition o barkin!'

Itchcock's Brother

My missis an little daughter
wen inta Walter's Photos down town.

Totelee gobsmacked when they seen im:
black suit an tie, a white shirt
like ee wuz a fewnral director
cept ee wore a white wig
ad a cushion stuffed down is trousers,
sunglasses jest like a gangster,
with a stand-out sign
angin round is neck
proclaimin 'DAVID HITCHCOCK'.

'Cun yew take my photo, love?'
ee asks the shop girl.
My little daughter goes up t im –
'Oo are yew then?'
'I'm David Itchcock!' ee replies,
'brother of Alfred, the film director.'
(Meant nothin t my daughter . . .
now if ee's sayd Paddington Bear!).

I wern surprised when they tol me
coz I seen im loadsa times:
'MEXICAN DAVE' down Tescos
with is floppy sombrero,
'COWBOY DAVE' in is stetson
an 'POLICEMAN DAVE' down-a presink
with two proper coppers pissin theirselves.
An always the dangly placard.

So when she's older an readin
Film Studies at-a Uni o Merthyr,
my little daughter'll be able t boast –
'Alfred Itchcock, that great auteur . . .
yeah, I met is brother.'

Take'way Umpin

Ev'ry month we done it,
on'y arfter an Injun –
Chicken Tikka f'r er
Prawn Bhuna f'r me
(always-a same).

An we ad-a be pissed
so's we didn really see
each other proplee –
I ad six cans o lager
she ad a bottle o Lambrini.

Ev'ry month on a Fridiy
we ad it off reg'lar
like goin t church
or makin Christmas dinner,
or arguin bout the olidays.

I think it wuz good,
but I carn always remember –
she closes er eyes
an imagines I'm Tom Jones,
I close mine f Catherine Zeta.

Never got no ambition,
cept one time the Bhuna wuz off
an I ad to ave Vindaloo
an I got the squirts real bard
jest as we woz moanin.

Ev'ry month we got take'way umpin
an wha with-a recession
it could now be ev'ry season.
I ope she don' fall asleep on-a job agen –
slike she's goin inta ibernation!

Present t Myself

We're gonna ave fun later
me an my new fren,
pull a cracker or two t'gether.
She've dressed up as Santa
got black stockins on er;
a presen t myself.

Int nobuddy left,
I buried my on'y brother
an my sister thinks I'm weird.
My neighbours always say ello
an then I yer em larf.

My long mac angin,
my bobble at an spotty wellies
wha'ever the weather.
I yer them whisperin
through-a walls as I offer er
a leg o chicken.

'Sylvie!' I sayz, 'yew are
the one I bin waitin for!'
I wuz always too shy b'fore,
my tongue trapped, rabbit
in a snare; she shakes
er rubbery ips, got proper air.

My sister ad a doll once
er bes' presen, it even cried.
I flung it out-a window,
'Yew little bastard!' the ol man yelled.
I wouldn urt Sylvie ,
she's s soft an willin.
I lay er by-a Christmas tree.

Yew're Gonna Pay

'Yew're gonna pay f this,
sooner or later
gonna pay f this!'

Ee wuz a friend
o my ol man,
ee sayd don' worry
there'll be no rush.

But now I goh redundancy
an Christmas comin up
an I carn pay im back:
'Got frens,' ee sayz, 'not so generous!'

The debt's so 'eavy
slike cement on ower backs;
money runs through us
like-a Taff in flood.

An wassa big difference
between now an em truck shops?
The bailiffs'll be breakin down
ower doors with ammer-fists.

Christmas'll afto be cancelled,
my kids won' get nothin
on theyer Santa lists:
the future's a wall, no endin.

'On'y coz I know yewer dad!'
always a threat in is voice.
'Give yew till-a New Year
an en, take wha'ever yew goh!'

Me an my famlee below
an starin up, no cracks o light,
the shadow of-a wall
always blocks-a sun out.

'Yew're gonna pay f this, ol son,
yew're gonna pay f this!'

Owlin at-a Moon

It wuz New Year's Eve
at-a Venue,
on'y the place is called
'I Can't Believe It's Not Buffalo's'!

Ardly anybuddy there early
jest-a ardcore solos
like myself with no place t go
no missis now
she've kicked me out,
though I still love er like mad.

S'many bard luck stories
yet we ad a larf
an I wen f'r a fag
in-a beer garden which is a yard.

Somebuddy sayz – 'It's a full moon!'
an we all gazed up
through the risin smoke :
a clear, cold night
an there it woz
bright 'n' round
as a promised coin
to a young child.

An this bloke, Mark is name is,
starts t owl like a werewolf
an we all join in
women an men, like we'd grown
air an ower fangs woz long.
An somebuddy from over-a wall
in-a bus station close by
owls a really loud reply
an we piss owerselves.

Tha's what I like about Merthyr:
this town's full o nutters.

Too Far Gone

Ee thought ee woz a kinda god
an we wuz is demons
tha night I'll never forget:
'I goh wings!' ee yelled,
'no way I'm gunna fall!'

We worshipped im, tha's a fact,
at school ee didn give a fuck,
ee give-a teachers loadsa jip
no matter ow ard 'ey made out.
Ee done anythin fr a larf:
cross-countree runs picked magies
swallowed em an tripped,
wen up Morlais Castle done a streak
an never made it back up-a school.

Ev'rythin borin t im 'cept art,
ee spent owers drawin
in practiclee ev'ry leeson;
in the end, teachers let im be,
long as ee kept is mouth shut.

Tha night woz ot as summer
though it wuz late September,
on-a bench by-a river
we slugged back-a White Lightnin,
loadsa stuff is bro ud bought.

As it goh dark we wuz loud as owls,
people in-a flats nearby tol us
t 'Shut it!' But Lee
ee shouts back – 'Oo, I'm shittin bricks!
Why don yew call-a pigs?'

An 'ey problee done it,
but with all-a fights down town
they never even come.
S we played dares an Lee
woz always-a first, o course.
By 'en ee wuz off is face
an slaggin off is ol man,
sayin ee'd fuckin kill im
f wha ee done to is mam.

S we dare im t climb across
an ol pipe: the river arf dry
an fulla eaps o stones,
pipe igh up, smooth an risky.

On'y when ee goh up an begun
is wobbly way did we realize
it wuz no joke, on'y when ee flapped
is arms an shrieked like a loopy parrot
did we shit ower pants an cry out –
'Lee! Come on mun! Come down!'

But ee wuz too far gone.
Nex minute ee slipped
onto solid boulders stickin out:
down like a bird shot
landin on is ead, never moved.

We panicked an done a runner.
Never even called-a cops.
Left im there t rot.
Now ee comes at me in nightmares
over an over, risin up
from-a river, crawlin up-a banks
an draggin at my legs,
pullin me down, wishin me dead.

Settin Fire t Tescos

Orright, I wuz off of my ead
on drugs an booze
the day I set fire t Tescos,
the day it rained in Tescos.

I tried t burn off-a tags, see,
t scurry through-a securitee,
when all ell let loose,
yew'd-a thought I wuz a terr'rist.

I done nickin before mind,
goh away with it loadsa times:
but I woz sober an clean 'en,
knew wha I wuz doin.

'larms begun t ring
like the panic o wakin,
sprinklers begun sprayin
water over ev'rythin.

Me an some o the staff
wuz chokin with-a fumes;
they soon catched old o me,
my ead a Waltzer spinnin.

I woz liftin clothes tha's all
coz I carn afford none:
arf my benefit goes to-a dealer
an the rest is jest f survivin.

What ope f the likes o me
when there's fuckall opportunities:
sirens blarin all over town,
theyer message – 'Goin . . . goin down!'

Soopermarkit Drama

Yew wouldn bleeve it,
I woz in-a soopermarkit
jest by-a frozen peas n carrots
when ev'ryone started goin mad.

'There's a bloke by there,
an ee's strippin off!'
'Ee's off of is trolley!'
(In is case, ee never ad one.)

I followed crowds an securitee
t where there wuz jeerin an jokin.
This young fella, beard an long air,
woz standin at-a top o Wines an Beers.

Too trew, ee wuz takin off is clothes
an urlin em down at-a crowd
oo cheered an clapped is striptease:
somebuddy sayz – 'Do-a Full Monty!'

Ee grabs old of a coupla cans
pops em and starts slurpin,
then ee wuz yellin – 'They charged me!
An I wern doin nothin!'

Before ee got down to is goolies
ee'd bin dragged down by eavies.
What a protest against shop-liftin,
ee wuz pissed with all ee'd bin nickin.

The On'y Way

Ee wuz a tidee teacher,
tol us stories,
knew wha ee bleeved in.

It wuz-a worse time f me,
parents always arguin,
fren's inta drugs n drinkin.

I coulda gone either way,
my ead like litter in a wind,
coulda ended up in-a drain.

Ee tol us Jesus wuz the on'y way,
t follow is life ev'ry day,
the bible ad-a truth of ev'rythin.

'I'm sorry, but gays . . .' ee'd say
'. . . ull all end up in ell
with anyone oo's disbleevin!'

At-a time when-a boyz
wuz inta glam, when bands
dressed up like women;

I knew ee'd saved me
an I'd leave my parents fightin
whenever tha Rapture come.

We done disgustin stuff in school:
'Of Mice n Men' all swearin an blasphemin,
this woman Angelou with scenes o rapin.

We ad meetin's ev'ry week at lunchtime,
ee tol us these wuz Satan's works,
the bible the on'y book of education.

We wuz the promised ones, ee sayd,
ee'd bin through it, drunk an misled:
English, I sat like a gravestone, an never read.

The Bloody Snow

I ate the bloody snow
t me its jest a nuisance now,
slike God's dandruff,
wish ee'd stop shakin is locks.

It's orright on cards
or when it comes an goes,
but stickin dayz on end,
ands an feet never bin s cold.

Pavements like slidy glass:
angin onto walls an fences,
my ol rag n bone body
worryin down t the bus-stop.

In-a soopermarkit mad panic
ev'ryone's buyin undreds o loaves,
they mus be off theyer trolleys,
I on'y bought ten t freeze.

Tha's all 'ey talk about in-a queues,
yew'd swear we woz Eskimos,
it's snow this an ice that
an ow it's warmer in Vladi-bloody-vostock!

All very well f kids doin angels
an snowmen an sledgin down ev'ry slope,
but f me it's getting my repeat
so's I don' ave a nasty turn.

I ate the bloody snow,
no matter ow many blankets at night
an wha will-a gas bill be like,
even-a sun carn make it go.

Fair play, some neighbours do ask:
'Need anythin? Milk or bread?'
Others dig theyr own paths,
eads down whenever I pass.

Diego Maradona Come t Merthyr

The day Maradona come t Merthyr
with is air totelee grey
an really short; is beer gut
ad gone all bigger.

The day Diego stands in-a Igh Street
goin on bout-a play-offs
an ow Cardiff blew it,
soundin jest like ev'ryone else.

The day ee lifts is And o God
an points down-a arcade
t where a new shop ave opened,
doubts ee've got any gold.

Slike some buildin society
on'y with-a name of a butcher;
in is blue n white stripes,
carn bleeve it's a pawnbroker!

With is face pale as lard,
with is worn out trainers,
numero 10 couldn elp wonderin
if is shirt ud bring any fuckin money in.

Surjree Talk

Funny ow, in-a surjree
ev'ryone always sayz –
'Yew orright 'en?'

Yew could ave yewer leg
bout t drop off, yewer skin
all covered over in sores;

yewer yers totelee blocked,
eyes bloodshot in agonee,
joints crooked with arthritis;

yew could ave yewer ead poundin
with-a migraine, nose streamin
an throat like a clogged chimley;

yewer eart bout to explode,
liver an kidneys pickled but not delicacies,
yewer goolies pocked with disease;

yew could ave all o these
an yew'd still bloody well reply –
'Not too bard, ow about yew?'

A Big Party

S' we decided to ave a Big Party
t celebrate-a Big Society
(it woz-a best way
t get on-a telly).

Better still, this bloke up-a street
woz comin back from Afghanistan
with a small wound on is leg,
so summin else t celebrate.

First time since-a Jubilee
and even them Thomases Welsh Nat's
Welsh-speakers never turned up 'en,
sayd they'd come along this time.

Ev'ryone ud be there cept Dirty Dick
number 69 done f flashin
all over-a local paper;
if ee come ee'd ave a good kickin.

It woz all ready, booze n buffet
(even cold pizza f'r the veggies),
journalist from-a 'Merthyr' with a camra,
but telly coverin a Big Orgy up-a Rhondda.

Never seen tha soldier before,
is mam wore a t-shirt sayin
'MAM OF A TOTAL HERO',
ee limped bard, toasted-a Queen;

Thomases started complainin in Welsh,
s' this eero Shane ee tells em –
'Fuck off ome t wherever!'
They jest sayd – 'We woz born in Merthyr!'

It did get better arfter tha,
we ad a Big Cake we all shared
and a Big Larf when some o the boyz
pissed all over Dick's garden.

Shane showed the kids is scars
an got to autograph a few girlz t-shirts;
it got barkin as the evenin wen on
with Big Drinkin Competitions.

Then Alan up-a road puts a dampener
on the whool bloody evenin,
stan's on-a table, one foot in-a cake remains
an gives off t ev'ryone –

'Big Fuckin Party!' ee shouts is ead off,
'yesterday I gotta Big News,
the Council's on'y laid me off
an now I feel like a nobuddy!'

Shane yells out - 'Yew should join the army!'
Thomases start singin '*Hen Wlad Fy Nhadau*',
I done a Big Spew in-a drain
an a Big Party become a Big Pandemonium.

In-a Bus Shelter

I woz goin f this job
over in Llanhilleth, see;
somewhere on the Mexican border . . .
well, a bit south o me.

They tol me all-a wrong bus numbers:
X18, E4, P45, UB40 an OMD,
Traveline Cymru up in a North Pole
an-a drivers didn know nothin.

At-a bus shelter I arst er.
She woz sittin an knittin
what looked like a jumper;
glasses an bright red air.

'Which is the one f Llan'illeth please?'
I sayz, careful not t gob over er.
'Cardiff?' she replies, in a voice deeper
an much oarser than mine.

She woz an *ee*, sittin there
in daytime with a shoppin bag,
as I repeated 'Llan-hill-eth!'
(Ee or she woz a Cockney.)

'Well, you can go to Aberbeeg an walk!'
Ee chwtshed at a baby in a pushchair,
never stopped knittin till is bus come.
Fuckin ell, Ebbw Vale's weirder 'an Merthyr!

Nothin Lager

I int no lager drinker,
but I ad no choice.

It didn taste o rat's piss,
it didn even taste o dog's piss.

It tasted o nothin at all,
not even bloody beer!

It woz cheap an alc'olic 'pparently,
but I couldn drink a pint ardly.

I kept thinkin a Cwrw Hâf an Braf,
of O1 an OHoHo an ColumbO;

I kept thinkin o Rhymney brews
made in a Dowlais micro.

I kept thinkin oppy an barley:
golden summer, bitter autumn, dark winter;

Spring in Belgium, with Trappist ales
t get any monk boppin.

But it tasted of all them chains
o the Igh Street, of metal links joined.

Passin Facebook Frens

I wuz goin shoppin down Cardiff
f'r a present f my mam
(Motherin Sundiy see,
an she lives on er own).

It woz then I kept noticin,
real weird, ow I kept on passin
one arfta another
s many Facebook frens.

Got loadsa frens on Facebook,
over a thousand I reckon,
an on'y a few of em
are buildin's an organizations.

More frens there for def
than I ever ad at school,
where I got called 'loner',
'loser' an 'real sad'.

Never looked up, busy on mobiles,
problee on Facebook or Twitter,
tellin frens they're shoppin,
or textin to actually meet them.

Couldn remember theyer names,
all my quick-passin Facebook frens;
couldn wait t get ome
tell them ow I'd mouthed 'Ello!'

Got on line an this woman
(ewsed t be at school), sends me a message
'Seen u down town'; I press 'LIKE',
check er Profile … intrest – 'SOCIALIZING'.

Fish Foot Clinic

It's come t Merthyr at las,
we got one o them 'Fish Foot Clinics'
down town in a posh stewdio.

In-a local paper it boasts
'Probably the biggest in Merthyr'
(far as I know, int no other!).

An orready I yeard 'bout this bloke,
pissed arfta goin up-a Wyndham
(one of-a top 10 ardes pubs in-a land);

ee goes inta this Clinic
where there's all these women
avin theyer feet nibbled by tiny fish.

'I wan mine done!' ee demands,
'on'y make it fuckin piranhas,
not them poncy fish yew do ewse!

Aye, they cun feed off-of my tattoos.
On'y piranhas are ard enough
f'r a pair o feet like these.'

'Sorry sir,' sayz the manager, thinkin 999,
'we on'y got these ones,
Gara Rufa 're gentle as yew please.'

'No way!' ee replies,' I'll bugger off
up a Chinese Ealth Shop an ave
loadsa needles stuck in my balls!'

Int Goin Out

I int goin out no more.
It int worth the risk.
This bloke ee got mugged in Merthyr
an it wuz on'y 8 in-a mornin!

I ewsed t travel t Cardiff on-a bus,
till this driver on-a News
runs inta somebuddy's ouse,
loadsa passengers woz urt.

Int gonna visit my bro in London,
too many knifin's an yew bet
Al Quaeda will pull off a big one
now tha they ad Bin Laden.

Cancelled my oliday t Tenerife
arfta tha pooer woman got killed,
ad er ead chopped off in a soopermarkit;
ee come out carryin it like a shoppin bag!

Bin thinkin o all em pit bull attacks
an tha girl struck by lightnin . . .
mind, she woz in er own ome.
I'll jest stay in bed an do nothin.

Mormons on a Mission

Ey, ave yew seen em
Mormons on a mission,
ridin down the ill
with rucksacks fulla scripture?

Theyer fast an freewheelin,
but they got theyer elmets on
jest in case ol Satan
ave got it in f'r them!

Ey, ave yew seen em,
name badges like executives,
the on'y cyclists with suits on,
Yanks ev'ryone one.

Theyer eyes straight a'ead
an ready t do convertin,
shirts white as virgins
(the on'y ones in town!).

Ey, ave yew seem em,
in pairs like window salesmen:
get yewer soul sealed with double glazin ,
get a tidee conservatree in eaven.

Criminal Fence

There are limits t bard language.
If I called ower neighbours BASTARDS
it'd an an insult t ev'ry child
ever born outa marriage.

There int words t describe ow I feel.
It should be summin like THATCHERS
or BLAIRS or maybe CAMERONS.
Wouldn wan t breathe theyer air.

It's ard t bleeve, they called-a pleece
three times in a matter o weeks,
they lied through theyer razor teeth:
they must ave a bloody ot-line!

Domestics, drugs, robbrees an may'em
all goin on round town,
but they come in seconds
all coz of a fence.

We come ome an it woz there,
a Bamboo Curtain, over six foot,
builders done it while we woz out;
my missis rippin, we took it down.

'Criminal damage!' sayz the officers,
'we could arrest yew on the spot!'
So we paid ev'ry penny t them
CAMERONBLAIRTHATCHERS.

Thought we owned the fence-posts
an got a builder t remove em;
agen the cops arrived like we wuz murderers,
talkin 'theft' arfta theyer lies on-a phone.

Third time it woz theyer builders
oo I tol wuz committin a civil offence;
when-a las cop come, thought I'd carried out fantasies,
sleep-walked an throttled em in my sleep.

No, this wuz about 'abusin the builders'.
If 'abusin' is such a crime,
they could arrest arf the population,
or make the whool countree a prison.

There are limits t bard language:
if I could really describe ower neighbours,
if I woz ever in-a dock
I think I'd call em VILE MURDOCHS!

Em'tied Lives

I done it all
f'r my famlee,
I worked all owers
an didn ardly see
my two little ones.

My missis workin on-a tills,
we paid f'r nursree.
It gutted me
t come ome late
an find em in bed orready;
I kissed theyer cheeks
an promised all-a olidays
we'd ave eventually.

It woz jest a letter,
I even joked t Debbie –
'If issa bill
put it where it b'longs . . .
in-a bin!'

I couldn bleeve it,
on'y a coupla months
we adn paid up:
wha with the eatin,
food goin up ev'ry day,
scrimpin f'r value stuff;
we don' even smoke,
go out on Sat'dys down-a club.

All tha talk bout 'negative equity'
'it me slap in-a face
like I'd bin mugged,
'repossession' a word
never thought I'd read
in a letter to us.

All-a thin's we'd done t the ouse
and I int even andy,
conservatory an a combi boiler.
Issa tidee area an all,
the kids cun play safely.

Don' know where we'll go:
my mam's is a small terrace.
She'd ave us tomorrow
but Deb is so cut up
she stares inta distance
an lissens when I rant –
'Whassa fuckin point?
Why ave we bothered?
All 'ese yers workin so ard!'

It's easy f them politicians
an them experts on-a telly,
sayin thin's ull turn agen,
sayin it's on'y tempree.
F'r us, it means ower lives
're em'tied, ower futures
stole like the bailiffs
come an took furniture away.

Wish now I adn toiled
my bollocks off doin overtime
an put the presen' first,
played with Shane an Faye,
read em stories till they slept.
An when Deb sayz
we'll afto start agen
I glare at er like she's crazee
like she aven learnt nothin.

On-a Bridge

Pass me by
on-a bridge,
I see yew go
with yewer bags,
come back full.

Yew don' see me,
I squat so low;
like dogshit on yewer shoes,
later scrape it off.

Walkway over-a road,
ev'ryone's goin somewhere,
but I got nowhere.
Carn offer no mewsic,
don' offer magazines.
I got nothin t please.

An emptee can
waitin f coins.
Yew turn away yewer eyes:
presen's t be bought
an ice on-a streets.

Ev'ry day I wonder
if the river an the weir
would take me further.
The cold an damp
got steel-capped boots;
theyer the ones oo stop,
an give me a kickin.

The stories

Bus-station Clinic

I knew the day Dezzy died tha the bus-station woz really a clinic. I shoulda worked it out before: arfta all, it woz the shape of a ewge 'C', as in clinic an also 'Casualty'!

I knew then tha each area of ower town ad its own purpose an the retail park woz the shape of two massive boxes f'r a reason. Above all, I knew tha right opp'site the Leisure Centre an new cinema woz the place where-a food junkies got theyer its: pizza, burgers, Sub's, wha'ever.

Dezzy musta bin waitin frages f'r is appointment there. Ee often lay in the numbered sections, all named arfta parts o the town. Ee never caught no buses far as I cun tell, an woz lyin on-a ground till one day ee jest closed is eyes an-a ambulance come.

Ev'ryone knew Dezzy an so did no-one. Ev'ryone greeted im an ee ad a larf with them. Arf the time yew couldn understan' a single word ee woz sayin, mind. All is words ud mumble inta one long river, like-a Taff in flood carryin loadsa rubbish along.

I ewsed t say to im – 'Orright, Dezzy?'

An ee'd reply – 'Izzammeredoffitoowsitgoinbut?' or summin like tha.

There wuz all sortsa stories 'bout im, but the local paper never really tol us the truth arfta ee snuffed it. It wuz all – 'People believed that he used to be a boxer', or 'Dezzy's real name was Desmond Foley and people have said he lost both his parents and never recovered.'

It woz all pewer speculation, wha's more I never actually seen im drinkin, but ee always seemed pissed as ell.

I woz there the day ee closed is eyes f the las time an I couldn do nothin. This young woman phones-a cops. This bloke oo wuz passin with a walkin-stick eld onto is wrist t check ee ad a pulse, but I jest stood there like a plonker!

I never even sayd to im – 'Dezzy, c'mon mun! Wake up!'

I watched till the ambulance come an took im away, but I knew ee woz a goner. Ee musta on'y bin 'bout forty odd, yet ee ad-a face of a 70 year-ol, one rotten tooth an woz mingin as an ol dog. Some people avoided im. Some youths ad pissed on im once when ee wuz sleepin, 'pparently. That wozn in-a paper. My mate tol me down-a pub.

From the day Dezzy died, I knew I adda do summin. Even though the bus-station woz a clinic, there wuz no sign o doctors or nurses there. All there woz, wuz this woman oo'd practiclee lost er voice, pickin up scattered bits o litter with a prong thingy. She talked t ev'ryone an woz a big mate o Dezzy. She let im sleep durin the day nex t the bogs an the chairs an tables where the off-duty busmen ad fags an a cuppa.

Anyone argued with er an they'd ave a pair o prongs to answer to! One gobby drive oo shouted at Dezzy t fuck off an kip in-a bogs where ee b'longed ad is goolies grabbed by them prongs. Ee never questioned er wisdom agen, I cun tell yew.

Anyroad, truth is I wuz lookin f'r a purpose in life. I'd bin made redundant few yers back at Ferraris up Irwin. I woz a bakin assistant there. My mate Jonesy ewsed t say – 'Ave they made yew a Master Baker yet? Yew always woz a bit of a wanker!' Ee as a way with words.

So with Suze (tha's the litterlady) as my Ead Nurse, I would fill-a gap an be-a Chief Doc of-a bus-station clinic. I decided t spend my dayz there doin what I never done t pooer ol Dezzy . . . summin.

I knew I wouldn ave far t go. Right on the edge o the clinic nex t the caff named arfta one of ower boxin eeros, woz the 'noculation area. This woz where ev'ryone come to sort theyer jabs. On'y thing 'bout these jabs is, while they do solve the problem o fatness, they also tend t turn people inta livin skellingtons.

I woz kitted out speshly f'r my first job, with an ol white overall an kiddies stethoscope picked up f'r a few bob in-a charitee shop. I knew tha since my missis ad done a runner with this bloke worked f the Estate Agents, I ad gone t pieces. I knew it, but couldn give a toss my air bein all straggly an my clothes ad begun t be as buzzin as Dezzy. Even so, I did try t clean myself up a bit. Washed under my armpits first time in months, though I never looked too close in case some kinda fungus woz growin there. I wern inta foragin!

I atto approach the Eadman o the 'noculation department an persuade im t start injectin summin else inta anyone oo paid im. Cabbage juice! Made it myself. It ud be much better than all tha stuff tha woz turnin the patients inta walkin corpses.

I spent long enough in-a clinic previous t know oo ee woz. I soon located im right by-a news kiosk collectin a wad o dirty tenners from one of is patients in exchange f medicine.

'Scuse me!'

'Whadda yew wan?'

Ee eyed me up real suspicious.

'This is the 'noculation department, right?'

Ee larfed an called out to is girlfren.

'Ey Kar . . . come yer! This bloke wan's a tetanus jab! Ee's fuckin off it!'

Is girl Kar come over an jest starts pissin erself, like I wuz totelee barkin.

'Nah, I'm serious! D'yew wanna ave summa this? It's good stuff! Really ealthy . . . inject this inta people an it'll give em a real boost.'

When I eld up my jam jar fulla cabbage juice, Kar cackles, but ee looks at me more squinty-eyed, like I wuz up t summin.

'Wha is this, some sorta scam? Yew work f'r the pigs or wha?'

But Kar brung im down t earth sudden.

'Wise up Rich, ee don mean nothin. It's problee snot

juice, in it?'

'Snot juice? 100% cabbage. Full of iron. Adds 10 years t yewer life. Guaranteed!'

This Rich pins me up 'gainst the wall an talks real slow an deliberate.

'10 fuckin yers dildo-face! Oo wan's 10 more fuckin yers?... The whool idea is to ave less bleedin time not more, an t blank it out not drum it up with fuckin iron brew, wha'ever.'

I couldn argue with tha. Ee obviously knew is patients better than me, an there they woz sittin on-a wall draggin at fags ev'ry few seconds an waitin f the nex chance t get a jab. My cabbage juice woz a total failure, but Kar musta seen summin in my face, coz she sayz –

'Tell yew wha love, we'll take some!'

'Wha the fuck yew on?'

'Ev'rthin Rich! Yew know me! . . . There's no arm, is there?'

So I give Kar the jam jar an returned ev'ry day t theyer department, but nothing changed. Rich woz still doin is business, patients disappeared inta the nearby bogs an Kar woz always angin round gettin thinner an thinner. The line o smokers woz always there, ready f theyer reg'lar 'ppointments.

I decided to abandon them no-opers f my nex task. So's t win over Suze, the litterlady, I'd need a tidee scheme. I'd always bin a bit of an inventor, but the missis wuz never impressed. I once made summin t make ower sex life easier an she lost it.

'I'm not wearin tha, Kevin Dyer! It looks like a bloody chastity belt!'

If on'y, I thought. *She wuz problee bonkin er Estate Agent by then, so it woulda come in andy.*

'It's meant t be a 'lectric stimulator . . . get yew goin like.'

'It smells o friggin fish!'

'Could be burnin!'

'Burnin? Yew tryin t set me alight down below, coz tha's the on'y way . . .'

'No, no . . . I jest done trials tha's all.'

'On what, exac'ly?'

'Jessie!'

'What? Yew are totelee loopy! . . . I thought she wuz walkin funny . . . yew oughta be locked up!'

Jessie woz ower mongrel bitch. The missis took er when she done a runner. Didn trust me, obviously.

I do know Suze, but not particlee well. She ewshly croaks 'Hiya!' at me, while prongin a stray can at my feet.

When I approached er I woz wheelin the prototype, Recyclo I. I wuz real proud of it.

'Suze! Wanna job?'

'Wha? I gotta job! Carn yew see I'm doin it!' er voice crackin like a scratched ol record.

'Nah, another job! Yew could be my nurse yer, now I'm Chief Doc. I'm gonna sort all these sick people.'

She stopped prongin an stared me full face, like I wuz from another planet. She grinned.

'Ow much yew gunna pay me then?'

'Nothin! But yew get the first ever Recyclo f free!'

'Wha's one o them when it's at ome?'

She carried on pickin an baggin bits 'n' bobs, as I pulled up the black bag t reveal it.

'Dar-arm! . . . I made it like a shoppin wheeler, on'y it's got three sections . . . cans, paper an plastic.'

She examined it with er prongs, expectin it t collapse, which it never.

'Ow the ell's this gunna elp?'

'Well, yew ewse it, an anyone with a walkin stick . . . arf the town I reckon . . . cun get one from yew.'

'Sorry t seem like them Dragons' Den but . . . I'm out! I got my prongs an bag an till the Council tell me different . . . no chance!'

'There's a bag at-a back f shoppin. People could elp the

environment an get about ...'

But Suze woz amblin off along the clinic corridors by then. An ol bloke with a metal stick come towards me.

'Yer but, ave this an ditch yewer stick!'

'What is it, son?'

'It's f shoppin an recyclin.'

'Sorry! I aven ridden no bike frages.'

Couldn even give it away, so I dumped it in-a river 'long with-a shoppin trolleys an plastic bags. Jest one more scheme. One more attempt.

I racked my brain f dayz. Come up with this device screwed onta the belly-button an looked like the top of a beer-barrel, but it woz too risky. In the end, I wen f summin a lot more easy.

Got my little table an chair from-a shed, scraped off-a slugs, bought some face paint an made a fancy sign:

DOC DYER
BELLY PAINTER
HE'S A ONE OFF!!!!!!!

In my frayed white overall an plastic stethoscope, I set up my stall on-a path which run 'cross-a grass nex t the bus-station. I chose Market Day coz it wuz eavin.

Loads walked this way to avoid bein dive-bombed by pigeons. Suze come out t see wha I woz up to.

'Now wha yew doin, Kev?'

'Belly paintin! Need yewers done?'

'I wouldn let yew near mine fr a million pounds!'

She moved on, er larfter like a fire jest bin lit. I'd ave t get another nurse. No commitment, see.

Famlees passed an the kids tugged theyer mams towards my stall.

'Mam, cun I ave my belly done?'

'Shut up, Chelsey, ee's a nutter!'

Charmin! No respect f the medical profession

nowadays.

Eventually, 'bout lunchtime, this loada blokes come along, rat-arsed as ell. They never seemed no bother at first, jest gathered round avin a giggle.

Then I recognized one. Known im at school, three yers younger an a real pain. Ee ad a real talent f windin up others t pick on me. Still ad, coz ee kept eggin on this ewge bloke t try my belly paintin.

'Go on, Scripo, give it a go! Yewer missis'll be well impressed! Yew cun do belly-dancin f'r er!'

An all the others join in, encouragin.

This Scripo woz bloody enormous. Looked like ee wuz expectin twin elephants. Ee collapsed onta my seat an I thought I yeard it breakin. Ee adn really focused on wha woz appnin, but when the others tol im, ee lifted is t-shirt t reveal a massive tump o gut.

'Wha d'yew wan on it?' I arst.

Ee gazed round, ead spinnin an eyes glazy.

'Ow 'bout a dragon!' sayz Lee, the one oo wuz at my school.

The others made stewpid suggestions like – 'Ow 'bout a pair o tits so ee cun feel hisself?'

'Ow 'bout a face . . . if yewer missis is ever doin a blow job, she'll ave someone t talk to!'

'I carn do a dragon, but I cun do summin bright an colourful!'

'Yer tha Scripo! Yew'll ave a fuckin rainbow on yewer beer-gut!' Lee sayz.

'Ow much?' slurs Scripo.

'Totelee free! It's on-a National Ealth!'

They all pissed theirselves.

It took me ages coz Scripo kept wriggling an complainin it tickled.

'Wha is it, a ball?'

'I reckon it's Scripo's ead!'

I done a blue balloon on-a string, with a message on

sayin – 'Let me free!'

Most o them blokes jest ad a larf, but when Scripo come to examine it, ee wern appy.

'What the fuck's this mean?' ee seemed t sober up sudden.

Seen Lee messin with my paints – 'Sayz yer these're permanent, Scripo! Yew're stuck with tha b'loon f'rever!'

I don think they woz. Ee problee made it up.

'Bloody bollocks!' roars Scripo, standin up.

The nex thing I know is total blank. It woz like somebuddy ad shot me in-a fore'ead. I woz down-a mine, no lamp, splutterin f breath.

When I come round, I wuz bein carried on a stretcher an Suze, fair play, woz over me with a bit of ol cardboard fannin my face.

The ambulanceman musta bin surprised t see me open my eyes. Ee musta thought I'd done a Dezzy, 'cept I ad blood streamin down my face.

'What appened but?'

'It's orright! I'm a doctor!'

'Must ave concussion,' ee tol Suze,'ee's totelee delirious!'

They on'y come t pick up-a bodies, I thought, *when it's too late.*

In-a ambulance I come round enough to ask the man – 'D'yew remember Dezzy?'

'Dezzy? Course I do! I remember im before he woz on-a streets. Is missis left im with is on'y boy . . . wen t London or summin . . . ee lost it arfta tha.'

In-a ospital it seemed more like a bus-station, everybuddy in queues waitin t go somewhere. Glad I woz on wheels an whizzin past.

I atto invent summin quick, summin t stop me goin the same way as pooer ol Dezzy. Some machine tha would put the brake on my down'ill brain, send it risin up like a satellite.

Screwy

There's a bangin on the door and I know it's im; it's Screwy. Ee seems t think tha jest because I tol im about the tree I like im. But I don'. It seems weird thinkin of im with tha nickname. Before it append it woz plain 'Rich', or even 'Richard'.

Go away! Don' answer the door, mam! Ee's a pest! Ee's crazee!

I know wha tha word means now: crazee. Ee woz always like tha an yew couldn get away from it. Ee lives opposite, see. As I leave f'r ower school up the road, ee inevitably tags along, jabberin 'bout is latest obsession. I'm o'ly quarter lissenin.

'Jon, Jon! Yew gotta get one! It's great! Yew cun practice out the back. I even made oles in the grass.'

'Rich, I carn stand rabbits!'

'Golf, Jon! I'm talkin about a golf club!'

Golf? I mean, ooever yeard of someone ower age playin golf? Yew've got to be over forty with a cardigan patterned like a table-cloth! Yew've got to ave loads of money t get more than the one club Richard ad.

But from tha day on, it woz all pars and birdies, tees and bunkers. I picked up on the terms, but paid no attention t what 'ey actually meant. Richard ad put me off the game for life. Even if I become the leader of some big company like Pizza Ut (an that ud be eaven, bleeve me) an ad plenty o time t go round the courses . . . what woz they called? . . . links? . . . Even if I achieved tha, I'd never raise a club, or join one f'r tha matter.

Ee wuz the same when this new teacher come to ower school. It woz a funny time for one t start, in spring, but ower las teacher ad left suddenly with er nerves. This teacher woz different. For a start, ee woz a man. Secondly, ee woz mad about local istree. Ee tol us ee wozn from round yer an this made im all the more interestin. In fact, ee woz to istree what Rich woz t golf: a fanatic (I know wha tha means coz my dad tol me 'fan' comes from it).

Mr Twiss ad a peculiar English Coronation Street sort of accent, but seemed t love everythin about ower area. Personally, I didn get it an made the mistake of tellin him.

'It's jest a load of ol ills with grass growin over em!'

'Jonathan, Jonathan! I don't believe you, old chum! Look more closely the next time you go out on that land and play . . . what are you into . . . golf, is it?'

See wha I mean? Richard an im must ave bin telepathic.

'Those hills are tips grown over. For every tip there was a mine . . . well almost. You're talking drifts and small shafts here, Jonathan. Later on in the week I'll take the whole class out there and explain.'

Drifts and shafts. Woods an irons. I felt lost as the rest seemed t wait on is ev'ry word. Ee wuz tall an the girls all thought ee wuz lush. I spotted two warts on is face the first day ee ad us: they woz like them tips. An ee'd called it 'the land'. Didn even know it was the Waun. Ee wozn so clever, despite wha ee'd read.

The next day walkin t school, Richard ad abandoned golf. Ee'd bin up all night surfin the net, is mine of information.

'It's fascinatin, Jon. Mr. Twiss woz right. Yew should look into it. There's even a ruined chapel out there . . . Cwmglo . . . it woz ewsed by . . .'

'I bin there!'

'Yeah?'

'Yeah. It's jest a pile of ol stones!'

'Oh My God, Jon! I carn believe yew! It's one of the earliest examples of Dissenters' chapels ...'

'Shut it!'

'What?'

'I said shut it, Richard, an go back t yewer bunker. It's mega borin all this istree stuff.'

Tha day in school, Twiss give us a lecture on the Merthyr Risin of 1831. It wozn a riot, ee explained. My brain was riotin. All tha rubbish about 'truck shops'. I couldn work out why they woz sellin lorries in Merthyr back then. An there wuz all these soldiers surroundin the Castle Cinema, of all places. I thought of it, boarded up an closed down with these rich iron makers inside, among the old cans and sweet wrappers.

To my orror, I found myself gettin drawn into it. I woz tol to act the part of a bailiff an Twiss chooses Catherine Jones to be an ol lady. This woz the best bit. As she slept on two chairs, I got to pull 'em from under er an she fell to the ground screamin. It musta bin dead good bein a bailiff in them days. I lost it arfta tha when they all seemed t turn into vampires, pourin lamb's blood into a bucket.

At break, Richard woz a pain. As I woz kickin a ball round with the boys, ee come over, full of it.

'See Jon, I tol yew. It's great, innit?'

'Wha?'

Ee wuz beamin, as if ee'd won.

'All tha istree. It's like time-travel really.'

As I stared into is animated face, the nickname 'Screwy' begun t take shape.

'Eh? Bloody Twisted more like.'

Ee peered at me, shocked. To im, I'd sworn about God. Chrissy Phillips wellied the ball over an it it Screwy on the ead. I guffawed.

'Great ead, Rich! Yew should be striker f the school team.'

He sulked away. If he tol Twiss . . .

Next day, Mr. Twiss continued with is story about the Merthyr Risin. There woz summin about settin fire t coffins an ev'rybuddy wantin bread an cheese. They musta bin avin a picnic up Dowlais Top where the march started.

Worst of all woz when ee tol us about one of them Big Iron-makers gettin theyer workers anged or sent to Australia. It woz then tha twti Paul Unter, who wuz always chirpy, broke down cryin. Ee wuz inconsolable. Eventually, Twiss got it out of im tha is dad ad jest lost is job. We all knew is dad worked up the iron works at Ebbw Vale.

'A terrible coincidence!' declared Twiss.' We're all really sorry for you, Paul. I'm sure he'll soon get another job.'

Paul-O, as we called im, kept to imself at lunchtime, which woz strange f'r im. We let im be, waitin till ee wanted t join in agen. Everyone, tha is, 'cept Screwy. Ee couldn resist it an wen' straight up to Paul-O , ammerin questions like ee wuz investigatin a crime. Yew could yer im a mile away.

'I carn believe it! It's weird!' ee wuz sayin. 'Yewer dad's an ironworker, right?'

Paul-O jest nodded glumly, tryin t turn away.

'What's is name?'

'Mr Unter!'

'No, I mean is first name?'

'Lewis, Lewis Unter.'

When Screwy yelled out summin in Welsh sounded like 'Losin a Ell' I'd ad enough. Pooer ol Paul-O woz on-a verge of blubberin, so I stomped over.

'Leave im be, Richard! Yew're makin it worser!'

But Screwy ad this mad glare on im.

'Don' yew see, it's more 'an coincidence . . . it's all

appenin agen.'

Tha oz it!

'Yew gone totelee screwy, yew ave! Screwy Lewy . . . tha's what yew are from now on!'

I give im a shove an before I knew it arf the yard woz round us chantin, 'Fight! Fight! Fight!' Ee fell backwards onta the ground jest t make it seem more dramatic an Miss Jones appeared from nowhere t drag me away.

The Ead Mr Williams give me a real tellin off, circlin round me in is office, like the Bard Cop on telly. Ee wouldn lissen to no reasons, an called them 'excuses'. I tried t tell im I woz defendin Paul Unter .

Now I atto get revenge on Screwy, sooner or later, but preferably sooner. I'd wait f r the moment an strike.

The nex day woz ower trip t the Waun an if I didn be'ave I'd miss it. Big deal, I thought, I knew it better 'an ower garden. On the other and, it'd give me a chance.

In the mornin ee ad the cheek to cling onta me on my way t school.

'It's orright, Jon. I accept yewer apology.'

'I never said sorry.'

'Yeah, but yew'll afto sooner or later or yew'll be doin lines instead of goin onto the Waun.'

I woz about t throttle im on-a spot, but decided t be sly.

'Yeah, yew're right Scr . . . Rich. I shouldn of pushed yew so ard.'

'Tha's okay! I won't tell Mr Twiss!'

'What about?'

'About yewer nickname f r im, of course. It isn't nice.'

'Yeah, yew're right! Best keep quiet.'

Inside I woz seethin. The nerd! The creep!

In class, Twiss tol us about this bloke Dic Penderyn. I woz glad it wozn me tha snortled at the name 'Dic', but

Natalie Evans, oo wuz about a foot taller than any boyz an wore bras the size o kites!

'Natalie, really!' But Twiss still ad a twinkle in is eyes.

I woz lissenin closely, ready t try an impress im arfta yesterday. Apparently, this Penderyn woz a 'merthyr' which means 'martyr' in English an ee wuz ung on-a steps of the libree down town. Ee wuz innocent (jest like me tryin t stand up f'r Paul Unter) an still adn got a pardon off of the Queen. Some said Penderyn ad idden on Aberdare Mountain, which woz the name Twiss now give t the Waun.

Then Twiss totelee spooked us out.

'Dic's real name was . . . Richard Lewis!'

Ee on'y glanced at Screwy, oo grinned proudly an nodded to us like ee'd known all long (which ee problee ad).

I spen' lunchtime goin through the motions of footie an Chrissie woz fed up of my quarter-hearted play an threatened t put me on-a transfer list.

'I seen trees move more 'an yew!'

I woz thinkin of a plan. My idea took root, but I'd wait t carry it out.

'Thanks, Chrissy!' I said, an ee stared at me as if I ad branches growin from my yers.

Tha afternoon, as Twisted led us out onta Aberdare Mountain, I woz itchin t try it out on Screwy. At first ee stuck to Twiss like Blu-tack. Ee ung on ev'ry word as the teacher tol us ow Penderyn got caught up in-a violence an woz accused o woundin a Constable somewhere by Wetherspoon's pub (which woz named arfta im).

'Merthyr aven changed much, ave it sir?' Natalie butted in. 'My brother got into a fight down there las week. The cops come along an . . .'

'Thank you Natalie!' Twiss shut er up jest as it woz getting intrestin.

Gradually, I managed t get Screwy away from the rest by askin loadsa questions. Ee wuz amazed I'd become so fascinated all of a sudden an we walked be'ind the others.

'Think of all them people, Jon, facin up to them Scottish soldiers sent from Brecon.'

All I could imagine woz Chrissy's comments about secret weapons up theyer kilts, but still nodded like a car poodle.

The Waun's divided by quite a few streams. Although they're small, theyer banks're steep an overgrown with oaks, briars, bramble, gorse an bracken. As Twiss an the class disappeared inta the trees an bushes, me an Screwy lagged be'ind. Ee wuz prattlin on about some guests an bacon an I couldn see what it ad t do with the Risin, but daren't ask.

'Now!' I thought, sudden as a gunshot.

'Ey, Rich!' I stopped an stared down'ill, like I seen a ghost.

'Wha? What is it?'

'D'yew know, jest down there . . . I found this tree, see, an . . . my dad reckons tha's where this Dic Penderyn id when ee woz up yer, coz it's an oak an ollow . . . bet yew could find it an really impress Mr Twiss, eh?'

'Wow! Really? . . . Shull we go an look for it?'

'Tell yew what, Rich . . . yew go down there an I'll go an tell Mr Twiss where yew've gone, right? I bet ee'll get ev'ryone t follow yew.'

'Onest? D'yew reckon?'

'Yeah, I'm shewer!'

'Where is it then?'

'Jest down by the stream. Right opposite the ol ropeswing.'

'Cor! Cool! See ya!'

'S'long . . . Screwy!' I ushed is nickname as ee opped off

among the bracken like tha rabbit in 'Alice'. Ev'rything woz goin accordin t plan an I urried t catch the others.

They ad all gathered by the stream lissenin t Twiss or lobbin stones.

Chrissy smirked, 'Why woz yew talkin t the geek?'

'Oo, Screwy? Ee kept goin on . . . anyway, ee run off.'

'Wha? What did yew call im?'

'Nothin! . . . ee jest done a runner. Said ee atto see summin.'

Twiss' voice woz loud over the sound of the gurglin water.

'Just think kids, this could have been the very spot where Penderyn washed his wounds after the Rising . . . Jon, Christopher, try to pay attention please!'

Chrissy responded as if I woz workin im, boundin down the bank like a pantin puppy.

'Sir, sir, it's Richard Lewis, sir . . . ee's . . . ee's . . .'

'Now calm down, Christopher . . . whatever is it?'

'Richard's done a runner!'

Twiss' eyes begun t twitch round the class.

'Rich-ard! Rich-ard!' ee called out, as though ee woz idin on purpose. 'Oh my God!'

While I reminded Twiss tha Richard's dad woz a Governor an Natalie explained ow there woz great places to ide on the Waun – as she'd found out with er lates' boyfren Lloyd, oo wuz fifteen – the teacher begun t panic.

'Who saw him last?'

'It woz Jon!' declared Chrissy.

Ee grabbed me by the arms an almost lifted me to is face.

'Jon. Which. Way. Did. He. Go?'

'Sir . . . put me down!'

'Okay, okay!'

'Sir, ee wen' that way!' I pointed downstream, 'ee wuz

mumblin summin 'bout the rope-swing. I ope ee aven done nothing stewpid!'

Now Twiss woz shakin an wuz ghostly pale. I pictured is mind speedin fast forward as ee snapped orders.

'Right, everyone follow me and hurry up, will you? Mark, stop hitting that tree!'

Ee stomped along by the stream, gettin really frustrated when the path run out.

'Sir, I know the way . . . I spent ages on the Waun.'

Ee eyed me in desperation, 'Alright, Jon! Go on, you lead the way!'

I tramped up the bank an through the bushes, a windin route of animal tracks. All-a time Twiss called out t Screwy, like a farmer lookin for a lost lamb. I knew exactly where we could skirt the banks, comin down the slope to the ollow oak where Richard could be concealed, imaginin ee wuz Dic Penderyn imself.

'The rope-swing's down by yer, sir! Maybe ee's avin a go on it.'

Twiss let out a bellow an I could follow is thoughts like paths over the Waun. We glimpsed the stream agen.

'Richard!' ee yelled.

Right in front of us, Screwy leapt out from inside the large tree, like an owl in daylight. Ee woz wide-eyed as tha bird and gobsmacked, like we come from another century.

'I . . . er . . .' ee croaked.

Twiss strode down the dirt path towards the flappin Richard Lewis. If Screwy coulda taken off an id in the trees above ee woulda done.

'Richard! What is going on?How dare you go off like that! I was extremely worried. Anything could've happened!'

'It did . . . I mean, sir . . . I seen im!'

By now the whool class woz boggle-eyed, totelee silent, waitin f'r is explanation. I expected im t turn on me, but ad my defence ready. But ee jest carried on in this weird slow voice.

'Sir, yew're not goin t believe this, but I think I seen Dic Penderyn's ghost. Ee wuz angin on the rope-swing an ee shouted summin in Welsh, I...'

'O Arglwydd dyma gamwedd!... O Lord, this is injustice!' Twiss boomed.

'Yes, that woz it, I'm shewer...'

'Penderyn's words as he was on the gallows,' Twiss gazed sympathetically at Screwy now.

'I did, sir... I definitely seen im!'

'Screwy,' I muttered, 'really Screwy.'

'What was that, Jon?'

'Nothin, sir.'

Twiss approached Screwy, pattin im on the ead like a dog returned to is master.

'Look, Richard, yew probably went to sleep. You had a dream. You've been reading so much about...'

'No sir, I didn... it woz im... it woz is spirit!'

From tha day on the nickname stuck. Ev'ryone called im tha, not jest me. But in typical Merthyr fashion, the more I tried t make it an insult, the more it become a mark of admiration. On the way back t school even Natalie ad noticed im.

'Yew're mad, yew are... mad as f... sorry sir!'

Even Chrissy woz taken in.

'Wow Screwy, a real ghost! Yew musta bin poopin yewer pants!'

Walkin ome I tried t question im properly.

'Nice story, Rich.'

'Story, Jon?... Don' yew think it's all a bit strange, eh?

My name . . . the ollow tree . . . the Waun.'

'I made it up.'

'What, about the tree? . . . Well, maybe yew didn.'

Ee had tha mysterious look agen. Owever much I tried t smear is name, Screwy remained 'The Boy Who'd Seen Dic Penderyn'.

I never returned t the rope-swing neither, f'r fear of seein summin.

Members of the Jury: What is your Verdict?

Arfta the game we ad a coupla pints and later my missis an is
. . . Mr Richards, my fren . . . joined us at-a Club. So, yes, I
adda few, I'd say ten or leven. An we woz walkin up the ill,
two of us in front, the women be'ind, walkin towards the
Chinese, it wuz bout leven. All of a sudden somebuddy
shoulder-charged me from be'ind! I it the wall, tha's ow I got
all them scrapes on my face yew cun see on-a photos. Ee
starts on Rye . . . Mr Richards . . . that is Jason Purnell over
there (I didn know im at-a time).

'Ey Army Boy! Think yew're ard, eh? . . . Le's go f'r it!'

I couldn yer nothin said before that.

'Le's leave it there!' Ryan sayz to im an I woz stood up by
then. I didn know nothin bout wha appened yers ago
between Ryan an is dad.

'Ey, tha's not on!' I sayz. I wuz gobsmacked.

'I'm gunna get my father!' ee shouts,' I'll be back!'

So we carried on walkin up the ill towards the Chinese
an within seconds ee wuz back an carryin wha I thought wuz
a knife. Comes at me with this blade so sudden I could ardly
protect myself. Ee stabs me real ard an I fall an old my ead. I
woz in-a daze an didn know wha wuz goin on, but Ryan ad
got im off of me some'ow.

'Yew'll ave worse 'an this!' ee yelled.

Ee run back down to is ouse down-a road. I never seen
im go into is ouse then, but I know now where it is.

Look! Ee knows wha ee've done wrong! Ee've ruined my
famlee. My ead wuz killin!

We went back down-a road t get elp . . . my rugby coach
lives down by-a Club. Aye, we walked back towards is ouse
an there woz some people outside there. Ee come out, no
top on an blarin at us an carryin this big kitchen knife.

'Yew'll ave some o this if yew int careful!' is what ee
shouted.

There wuz this car pulled up an one of em wuz a mate of is . . . I on'y know im as Spikey's son. They said – 'We'll phone-a pleece! . . . ewsin a knife, tha's not on!'

Yeah, they did tell-a pleece. I didn want no am'blance or f'r them t come, but that wuz earlier on, before I started bleedin all over-a place.

I wen straight up the ospital tha night. No, I never ad no stitches, but yew cun see in-a photo it wuz a stab, more like a gouge in fact. I wuz kept in till 'ey cleaned it up.

* * *

Me an Cath, tha's Ryan's wife , we joined the boyz f'r the night. I ad a few vodkas before we left . . . I'm not ewsually one f drinkin a lot. It wuz 'bout 'leven an we wuz walkin up-a road t get some food. I wuz in front an then the men, with Cath be'ind.

Ee come onto us from be'ind. We didn see nothin comin.

'Ey Army Boy, yew think yew're ard or wha?' ee sayz summin like tha. Then ee started on Ryan, but give my usban' Adam a shoulder-barge. Sent Adam flyin ee did. So Ryan starts oldin im off an I thought – 'Wha's is problem?' Ee seemed like one o them polar disorders t me.

Ee soon left yellin – 'I'm gunna get my father!' Ee wen down-a road.

We jest turned round an carried on, we wan'ed t get away. We didn wan no more trouble, speshly as ee seemed a bit of a psycho. But straight away ee come back an ee wuz swingin with is right and . . . with this thing I thought wuz a knife right at Adam, oo fell oldin is ead.

It all appened so quick . . . Ryan grabbed im an flung im inta the road,but ee run off shoutin: 'Yew'll get worse an tha! Yew wait!'

I phoned-a pleece. I stood over-a weapon . . . yes, it woz scissors jest like them. I tol the pleece that Jason Purnell woz be'avin strange an seemed like a bit of a psychiatrist t me.

The Boyz wen back down the ill f'r elp, back t the Club I think. I could on'y see bout one person outside is . . . Purnell's . . . ouse, but there woz this car b'there . . . two boyz in it I think.

My usban adda go to ospital.

Ee knows wha ee've done to us!

I stood there till-a pleece come. Showed em the scissors. On-a pavement they woz.

*   *   *

Yes, arfta the game we wuz in-a Club, me an Adam, tha's Mr. Price. We ad a quiet night with a Girlz, nothing speshul. I ad a few pints . . . maybe eight or nine, ewusual f'r a Sat'dy night.

Cath (my wife) an Donna (Adam's wife) joined us later on. We left about eleven t go up the Chinese up the road, get some food t take back ome. Over ower ouse, not far inta town. We walked along, the women in front, men be'ind. An arf way up I yeard a shout. I turned an reco'nized im . . . it woz Jason Purnell . . . I seen im down-a Club a few times. Knew im from way back. There wuz this incident with is father . . . tha's why I joined the army . . . it's all in the past now.

'Ey, Army Boy!' ee wuz callin out, 'yew think yew're ard or wha?' Summin like that.

An Cath, my wife . . . yes, she did say summin back. I carn remember what. Nex minute ee barged inta Adam, sent im flyin an I stood in front of im.

'Look, there's no need f that!' But ee looked really aggressive, like ee wuz out f trouble. Off ee went sayin ee wuz goin t fetch is dad. We carried on, jest opin it wuz all over, but seemed like 10 seconds an ee wuz back an carryin summin, looked like a knife.

Jest as ee wuz bout t take a swing at Adam, I wrestled im t the ground. We wuz on-a road an I wuz tryin t old im down an Adam come t elp. Ee swung up at Adam with is right, caught im with-a blade on is ead. Adam fell back bleedin. I wen t see ow ee woz an Jason Purnell got away, all-a time yellin stuff like – 'I'll ave yew!'

We on'y wen down is ouse coz it woz on-a way. We wuz lookin f'r elp. There wuz all these people outside is garden, some of em from-a Club. Ee come out arf-naked an holdin a bigger knife, a kitchen knife I'd say it woz. Ee then made more threats to us, but I carn 'member is exact words. These two boyz in a car said they'd phone a pleece. I didn know em, but since then Adam . . . Mr Price . . . ave tol me one wuz Spikey's son, lives up by im . . . fren of Jason Purnell's.

'It's not on, ewsin a knife', is what ee said.

*   *   *

We met up with the Boyz at the Rugby Club. I on'y ad an arf of cider, I'm not a drinker. I wuz sober as a . . . forgive the reference yewer Onour.

We all left levenish t go for a Chinese, not far up the ill. We wuz walkin long, Boyz be'ind,me an Cath (Adam's wife) in front. It woz really quiet till I yeard im shout. I reco'nised im straight off . . . Jason Purnell . . . ewsed t live in-a same street. There wuz trouble yers ago between Ryan an is dad.

Before we knew it, ee'd shoulder-charged Adam. There wuz no provocation. I didn say nothin till ee started on Ryan an then I jest tol im t lay off it an stop draggin up stuff. Ryan warned im an ee run off yellin summin bout gettin is father an ee'd be back.

But within a matter of seconds there ee woz carryin summin, looked like a knife. Ryan grabbed im an there wuz a scuffle in-a road. I didn see nothin clearly arfter tha, on'y Adam screamin ee'd bin stabbed.

I seen a pleece car up-a road an me an Donna wen t look f'r it t get elp. Nex thing I seen wuz later, outside is . . . Jason Purnell's . . . ouse, when-a pleece wuz arrestin im.

Yes, ee didn have no shirt on. There wuz quite a few people gathered outside by then. I didn reco'nise most of em.

*　　*　　*

I'd bin down-a pub in the afternoon, ad a few pints. My missis an me ad a quiet night in, watched a DVD. Round eleven I wen up-a Chinese t get some food. I live in the ouse with my wife an son (oo wuz four at-a time). My wife wuz expectin then.

As I wuz walkin up the ill I reco'nised one o the people in front, Cath Richards. She ewsed t live in my dad's street . . . my dad lives in Barry now. Yes, ee lived there then an all. Soon as I seen er, she turned an started on me. She an I ad a few words before er usban Ryan (I seen im down-a Club quite a few times) tol me t shut it or else.

As I passed em, this Ryan jumped me an eld me down in-a road an as I struggled t get free this other bloke . . . the bald,fat one . . . yes, Mr Price . . . ee joins in. I jest grabbed the first thing I could see in-a street t protect myself. It woz them scissors there. They punched an kicked me while I wuz on-a floor. I swung them scissors up an musta caught im . . . Mr Price . . . on the ead . . . Yes, I'm left-anded. This worked coz ee backed off an eld is ead, but the other one . . . Richards . . . grabbed me by the t-shirt an I struggled t get it off t free myself. It musta bin ripped as I done tha.

I run off rapid back ome down-a road. I ad a really bard eye an my ribs wuz killin. I tol the missis t get upstairs with the boy an we shut the light off in ower bedroom. The pleece come later an arrested me. I tol them bout my eye, but they jest ignored it.

I wen up the ospital arfta I'd bin charged. Yew cun see them photos, I gotta black eye. I wuz passin blood . . . a renal injury, they said.

I never got no kitchen knife. I picked up them scissors. I never seen em before.

*   *   *

My usban Jason on'y ad a few drinks all ev'nin. Ee's not a big drinker. We sat in watchin a film. My son wuz downstairs with us, sleepin. Jase wen out fr a Chinese some time arfta eleven. Bit later maybe. When ee comes back quite soon, ee's all disturbed. Ee looked really upset. Never tol me what appened, but ee tol us t go upstairs an knock the lights off. I think ee wuz scared fr us t be onest.

No, we don' ave no kitchen knives at all. I never cook.

I wuz expectin at-a time. I neally lost the baby coz of all-a trouble, with Jason's arrest an ev'rythin . . . ee never done nothin an never bin in any trouble ever. Ee's tidee an always as bin. Ee've got a good job as yew know. I ad the baby premature . . . it woz touch an go!

I did notice is eye wuz in a state an ee didn have no shirt on . . . yes, tha's is t-shirt b'there.The one they found in-a street.

The pleece never took no statement off of me. There wuz people outside ower ouse when they took im away. I didn know most of em. They musta come from-a Club.

I couldn bleeve wha wuz appnin! Ee've never looked f trouble.

Acknowledgements

The story 'Members of the Jury, what is your verdict?' was runner-up in the 2011 Rhys Davies Short Story Prize.

A number of the poems and stories have appeared in the following magazines:
'The Interpreter's House' , 'Red Poets', 'Roundyhouse', 'Planet', 'the recusant',
The Robin Hood Tax anthology (ed. Alan Morrison).

The story 'Screwy' appeared in a previous incarnation as 'The Boy Who Saw Dic Penderyn' in the anthology
A Stone for Remembrance (ed. Barrie Llewelyn).

My personal thanks to M. Gustavius Payne for the cover picture and photographs.

Also published by Gwasg Carreg Gwalch:

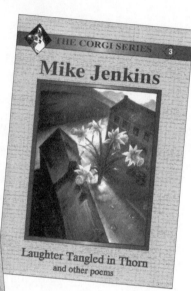

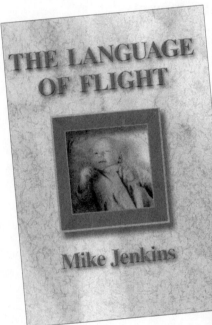

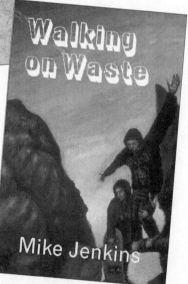